SURFING

WRITTEN BY SCOTT HAYS

ROURKE CORPORATION, INC.
VERO BEACH, FLORIDA 32964

PRO-AM SPORTS

The Rourke Corporation, Inc.
P.O. Box 3328, Vero Beach, FL 32964

Hays, Scott, 1959-
    Surfing / by Scott Hays.
      p. cm. —(Pro-am sports)
    ISBN 0-86593-349-9
    1. Surfing—Juvenile literature. [1. Surfing.]
I. Title. II. Series.
GV840. S8H39 1993
797.3'2–dc20   93-32164
                                  CIP
                                    AC

Cover photograph: Surfer Magazine (Jeff Divine)
Interior Photographs:
Allsport 12, 41 (Sylvain Cazenave/Agence Vandystadt)
California Office of Tourism 25
Surfer Magazine 4, 10, 16, 20, 21, 24, 27 (sequence),
    29, 30, 32, 36 (Jeff Divine); 5, 7, 14, 18, 23, 33, 34
    (Tom Servais); 28 (sequence); 28 top right
    (Lightwaves)
UPI/Bettmann Archives 9

Illustrations: Kasey Hinchman
Series Editor: Gregory Lee
Book design and production:
The Creative Spark, San Clemente, CA

Acknowledgments

Meg Bernardo. U.S. Manager for the Association of
Surfing Professionals in Huntington Beach, California.

Peter Johnson, General Manager of Rusty's
Surfboards and Accessories in San Diego, California.

Nick Carroll. Editor of *Surfing* magazine in San
Clemente, California.

Ian Cairns. Director of the Bud Surf Tour in Hermosa
Beach, California.

Printed in the USA

What can compare with gliding across the surface of the ocean? Riding the waves is what surfing is all about.

CONTENTS

CHAPTER ONE

Ride the Wild Surf — 5

CHAPTER TWO

All About Surfboards — 13

CHAPTER THREE

Getting "Tubed" — 21

CHAPTER FOUR

Surf's Up — 31

CHAPTER FIVE

An Endless Summer — 39

Glossary — 44

For Additional Information — 46

Index — 48

HOT TIP:
Want to know how to choose a surfboard? Turn to page 15.

There's nothing quite
like hitting the beach for
that first wave of the day.

Ride the Wild Surf

CHAPTER ONE

Toby and Jimmy walked down Main Street in Huntington Beach, California. It was early Saturday morning. Even the sea gulls were still sleeping. But for these two boys it was a glorious beginning to a perfect day. The surf was up!

They carried surfboards tucked under their arms. They wore wet suits to keep warm. Toby's was black with long sleeves and a splash of red. Jimmy's was blue with short sleeves and a splash of orange. They were only 10 and 11 years old, but surfing had become more than just a pastime. It had become a passion. They were already dreaming about becoming professional surfers one day.

They called themselves "Grommets"—young boys and girls who spend every waking hour thinking about surfing. If they weren't reading the surfing magazines, they were trying to get a ride to the beach.

When they reached the pier, these two Grommets sized up the waves with other older surfers who stood barefoot at the shoreline. The

The view from the water: waiting for a monster wave.

surf was giant. They entered the water. It was cold, but refreshing. They paddled out beyond the breakers and waited for a "monster" wave. Soon it was upon them. Both boys battled the forces of nature to ride the wild surf.

Toby hooked into a juicy section of the wave. He powered off the top and let the rolling motion take hold of his board. He quickly jumped to his feet and was at the wave's mercy. Jimmy came high *off the lip*, sliding down the *face* of the wave. He pumped hard on a clean four-to-six foot swell. Both boys went with the speed of a runaway sled down an icy peak. Their hearts raced with the thrill of the ride. It felt as though they were standing on top of the world.

After what seemed forever, the *white water* swallowed their boards and their ride came to a standstill. They gave each other a hearty whoop and paddled back out beyond the breakers to wait for the next wave.

A New Adventure

Surfing is unlike any other sport. The sensation of gliding down a wall of water will send your heart pounding and your mind buzzing with excitement. If you spend enough time around surfers, you will soon learn that none of them simply surfs for fun. Instead, they *sizzle*, *slash*, *carve*, *cut* and *shred* with passion and power. It's all a matter of attitude.

A true surfer is always looking for a bigger and more difficult wave to challenge. Facing one's fears is one of the attractions of the sport. The other is the outlaw charm that goes hand in hand with the lifestyle.

Surfing may look easy, but it's not. It takes hard work and a lot of practice. Standing on a board in shifting waters is a tough act. If you've never surfed before, it's a lot like skateboarding. Only instead of riding on asphalt, you slide along the crest of a wave. It's an exciting sport, and one of the most unique. But it can also be full of risks.

If you've been interested in surfing for some time, you're probably ready to learn how to hit the waves. The most important knowledge you need is how to read the ocean. The ocean is not like a tennis court or baseball diamond. It is alive and has its own set of rules.

Waves are formed by a combination of wind, currents and tide. They take shape far out in the ocean as a *swell*. As they move closer to the shoreline, they build to a point where they begin to break.

The dip in the water just in front of a wave is called the *trench*. The crest on top of a wave is called a *lip*. Once the wave begins to break, it forms a *tube* (or *barrel*). The ultimate goal of any surfer is to enter the tube and surround him or herself with a curtain of water. You may have seen pictures of surfers who look as though they are being swallowed up by a wave. They are *tube riding*.

Getting tubed—riding inside the curl of the wave—is the ultimate moment in surfing.

No two waves are ever the same. That's one of the fascinating things about surfing. Waves are perfectly natural, yet always uncertain. Even a small wave is powerful enough to push you and your board along at high speeds. But it can also push you under the water's surface against your will. This is why you should always be careful to choose the right beach and the right kind of waves. Waves that both form and crash on the shoreline are dangerous. The best waves are three-to-six feet high and start to break at least 30 feet from the shore.

If you become a good enough surfer, there's a chance you can turn professional. One of the youngest ever pro surfers was Kelly Slater from Coca Beach, Florida. At age 16, he won the Freestyle Inland Championship at Wild Rivers Waterpark in Irvine, California. At age 18, he won the Body Glove Surf Bout III. He also signed a contract with a sponsor worth an estimated $1 million and currently is world champion.

Some other top world surfers include Shane Beschen of the United States; Damien Hardman, Pam Burridge and Vanessa Osborne of Australia; and Sunny Garcia and Rochelle Ballard of Hawaii.

Maybe someday you will be as good as these surfers.

In the Beginning

Surfing started a long time ago in Hawaii. The Polynesians and some other South Pacific Islanders were the first athletes to stand on wooden boards in water and ride the waves. In 1778, explorer James Cook landed in Hawaii and described men who looked like they were "flying on water." The Hawaiians eventually introduced the sport to the United States mainland and Australia.

In the early 1900s, surfing went from an obscure sport to a popular one—due to surfers like George Freeth and Duke Kahanamoku.

Freeth was known as "the man who could walk on water." During the early 1900s, thousands of people would line the beaches in Hawaii and marvel at his thrilling surfing displays. He would stand on an eight-foot, 200-pound surfboard, wait for a large wave, and put on a sizzling exhibition.

Kahanamoku took up where Freeth left off. In August 1911, the 21-year-old Hawaiian broke an important world record by swimming through 100 yards of salt water in an amazing 55.4 seconds. Many people had a hard time believing it, but a newspaper reporter called Kahanamoku "The Human Fish."

One of the greatest surfers (and Olympic swimmers) of all time: Duke Kahanamoku.

He officially broke the world record in the 100-meter freestyle at the 1912 Olympics in Sweden, but surfing was his big love. So after his Olympic victories, he traveled around the U.S. giving surfing demonstrations. As a result, the sport began to attract a wider audience.

According to one legend, it was during the summer of 1917 that "the Duke" went for his longest ride ever off the shores of Waikiki. It happened on a beautiful summer's day. Huge, 30-foot-plus swells formed as the result of an earthquake in Japan.

As the story goes, the Duke surfed for at least a half a mile—from the outermost reefs to the shoreline. He later said of the ride: "I never caught another wave like that one. And now with all the birthdays piled up on my back, I know I never shall. Nobody will ever take the memory away from me. It is a golden one that I treasure, and I'm grateful that God gave it to me."

Is it any wonder that the Duke became known as the father of modern-day surfing?

The "woody" wagon was one of the earliest symbols of the surfer's lifestyle.

Modern surfing really started in the 1950s when an inventor named Robert Simmons made the first Fiberglas surfboards. These boards were lighter and less expensive than wooden ones. Then someone invented the wet suit, which made it easier to surf in cold waters. Before long, anyone could surf almost anywhere there was an ocean. People were riding waves on the east and west coasts of the U.S., in Hawaii, and as far away as Australia and South Africa.

The Surfing Craze

Legends like "the man who could walk on water" and "the Duke" caught the attention of both Hollywood and the music industry. In the '50s and '60s, Frankie and Annette cuddled on beach blankets during the night and surfed during the day. Gidget took up the sport to the delight of millions of Americans. The Beach Boys wrote songs about surfer girls and catching waves. Movies like "Five Summer Stories" and "The Endless Summer" captured special moments in a surfer's life. And the surfing craze had taken off like a rider off the lip of an awesome wave.

"When I first learned how to surf at 11 years old, I was one of the youngest people on the beach," says Nick Carroll, editor of *Surfing* magazine. "Most people didn't start until they were in their teens. These days, they're starting as early as eight or nine years."

Just go to any beach today to see how many surfers there are in the world. "Kids are starting a lot younger these days because their dads are surfers, too," adds Carroll. "Surfing used to have this image of an outlaw sport practiced by crazy young teen rebels, and to an extent that's still the case. But it's reaching a much wider audience. It's more of a family sport now."

Surfing gives you a feeling of freedom and excitement. But even more important, it feels like magic once you get the hang of it. Nothing can match the sensation of catching a wave and riding it for all it's worth.

Alone with just the wave and your surfboard, you will discover a new kind of freedom.

All About Surfboards

The only tool you really need to ride the waves is a surfboard. The first boards were built by the Polynesians and were made of wood. Later models were stained, dyed, rubbed with coconut oil, then wrapped in cloth. The best surfboards today are made of a lightweight foam and Fiberglas—a hard but flexible glass-like material.

Generally, surfboards are shaped like a flat cigar with the nose and tail turned up slightly. The two other major parts of a surfboard are the *deck* and the fins, historically referred to as *skegs*.

The deck is the top portion of the board that riders stand on. Skegs are located on the bottom. Today's boards use three fins or *tri-fin*, which help with steering and stability. The tri-fin also gives the rider the ability to do more tricks. They can be used on knee-high waves or on the biggest waves in the world.

Some boards are built for the size of the wave and geographic location. Smaller boards, for example, are used for average, everyday surf. Larger boards are designed for certain surf areas, and for bigger swells. In general, the bigger the wave, the bigger the board. There are many exceptions to this rule, however.

You can use almost anything to practice paddling and kicking, as long as it floats. A lot of young people start with plastic mats or rafts. If you're a little more experienced, you may want to try a *kickboard* or *bodyboard*. These will not prepare you completely for the demands of surfing, but are a good way to learn about waves and the ocean.

Over the years, surfboards have changed shapes. When the sport was first popular, an inventor named Tom Blake designed the first "hollow" board. He built it by accident when he tried to copy an ancient Hawaiian surfboard. On a whim, he drilled his wooden board full of holes to make it lighter. It worked.

Making surfboards has always been a painstaking craft, with builders experimenting with different materials and shapes.

He entered the board in the first Pacific Coast Surfriding Championship in 1928 held in Southern California. At first, people laughed. But the laughter soon turned to applause when he finished the 880-yard course by 100 yards.

Lighter boards changed the sport of surfing. In the late '20s and early '30s, inventors experimented with different sizes, shapes, weights and materials. Boards went from an average of 150 pounds to 75 pounds.

Steering and stability, however, were still a problem. Except for simple turns, the new boards were clumsy and hard to control. Eventually, Blake attached a fixed fin to the bottom of his board. This simple device gave him better control, making the sport more exciting for spectators and more fun for surfers.

Several years later, mad scientists Joe Quigg and his partner Bob Simmons built a surfboard made of Styrofoam and plywood. They covered the whole thing with Fiberglas and rounded the edges of the board to form *rails*. Before long, every surfer was using this new board design.

During the 1950s, surfboard builders began reshaping the noses, rails, and tails. Quigg built a smaller board for his wife and her girlfriends. Out of curiosity, he tried it out himself and liked it. He started doing tricks on the board that no one had ever done before. He was one of the first surfers, for example, to make a *radical bank turn*. It was the beginning of the end for the old-fashioned, crude surfboards. The new boards took on names like the Velzy-Jacob Pig, the Bing Pipeliner, the Bolt Diamond Tail, and the McCoy Single-Fin Cheyne Horan.

Over the decades, surfboard materials have changed, too. In 1958, builders started using polyurethane—a more flexible and rigid foam. New craftsmen entered the picture, including Hap Jacobs and Dewey Weber of Hermosa Beach, California, and Dave Sweet of Santa Monica.

The most creative surfboard builder, however, was Hobie Alter of Laguna Beach, California. He used polyurethane to build surfboards for his buddies in his father's garage. With a loan from his dad, he built a major surfboard business that he later expanded to include skateboards and sailboats.

As you can see, the history of surfboards includes new building materials, fancy designs, and a love of the sport. Along with these new models came styles of surfing like *air-whipping*. Surfers worked up new things on waves that were unheard of during the days of the Duke. When surfboards became easier to use and less expensive to buy, more and more people started surfing. And the sport grew in popularity.

If you're interested in learning more about the history of surfboards, you may want to visit a surfing museum. The Huntington Beach International Surfing Museum, for example, recently displayed some of Southern California's most historic surfboards. Visitors were treated to everything from a 1960s Batman surfboard to the only existing prototype of a longboard that folds in thirds and fits inside a suitcase.

BUYING A SURFBOARD

Once you've decided you're ready to surf, you need to select a board. If you're a beginner, almost any board that will allow you to practice paddling and kicking will work. Most people start with *longboards*, then graduate to the shorter, sleeker boards. A board that is too small tends to sink, while a board that is too big tends to be difficult for the beginner to control.

Buying a used board is a lot cheaper than buying a new board, but be careful. Sometimes a used board can have small cracks that will ruin your efforts at learning how to surf.

New boards usually cost from $375 to $450. They come in all shapes, sizes and colors. If you're confused by all the available choices, visit a surfboard store or specialty shop where someone will be able to help you and make some recommendations. Look through surfing magazines or talk to someone, perhaps a friend, who understands the sport. Let them help you pick out a board.

The proper way to carry your surfboard.

Bells and Whistles

Owning your own surfboard is fun, and it's even more fun when you start to decorate it with decals and stickers. You can find dozens of these items at almost any surfboard shop.

Of course, you shouldn't forget the other bells and whistles that go with your board and help round out the total surfing experience. These additions not only make you look good, but they help you ride better and more safely.

Most surfers, for example, own a *wet suit*. This skin-tight covering helps keep the body warm in cold water. A wet suit can cost from $90 to $300, and is a must in cold winter waters. The arms and legs of wet suits come in different lengths. Short sleeves and legs are good for fall and spring surfing, while long sleeves and legs are good for winter. During the summer you may want to wear only a wet-suit vest.

You'll also want to wax your new board to keep you from sliding off. Waxing the deck not only gives the surfer better traction, but it prolongs the life of the board by keeping water off of the surface. A surfboard is slippery, especially when water comes in contact with it. So you should apply a thin layer of wax just about every time you go surfing.

The best place to apply board wax is on the beach. You will eventually develop your own style of waxing. Some surfers wax the deck only lightly, while others wax it extra heavy in certain key spots. There's also a pad you can buy that has a peel-off backing. When it is applied to the deck, it works like wax in that it gives you better traction. These pads come in different sizes.

A cord or leash should be used to strap the board to your ankle to make sure your board doesn't hit someone in the head when you wipeout. It's usually attached to a leash cup on the bottom of the board. This device also keeps you surfing longer because you don't have to swim to the beach when your board gets there before you do.

Some surfing spots actually require you to wear a leash for safety's sake. If you do get hurt while surfing, a leash will keep your board nearby so you can use it as a life preserver.

Paddling gloves and surfing helmets are extras that aren't required, but they're a good idea. Paddling gloves enhance the power of each stroke. Surfing helmets are lightweight and come with an optional visor to keep the sun out of your eyes. They're both popular at certain dangerous surf spots, or when surfers are traveling to remote areas like Mexico and Africa and will be surfing in unfamiliar waters.

Many surfers will wear a wetsuit in order to stay out in the surf longer.

Surfers continue to experiment with new gimmicks to increase the thrill of the ride. One of the more recent fads is a foot strap that allows the surfer to get airborne and go ballistic. These fly-high surfers strap themselves to their boards and let it rip. "It's the feeling of not being limited to the wave but being unlimited in your imagination," says one surfer who uses foot straps. "It opens a whole new dimension to surfing: Air + Water = Insanity!"

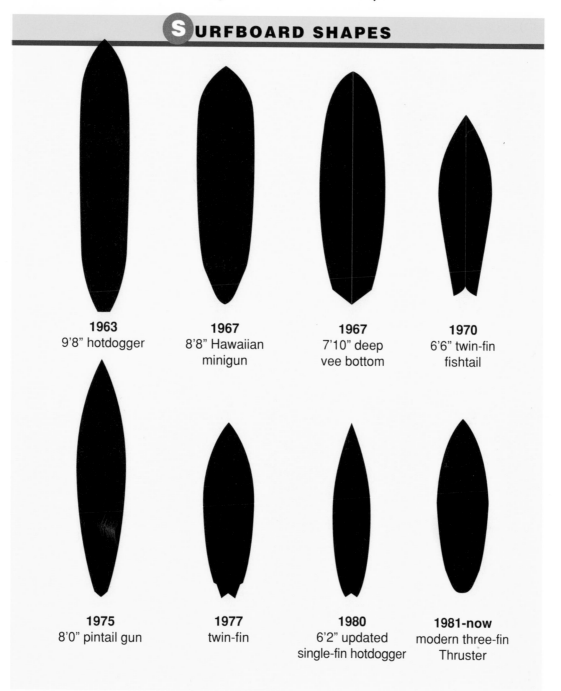

SURFBOARD SHAPES

1963
9'8" hotdogger

1967
8'8" Hawaiian
minigun

1967
7'10" deep
vee bottom

1970
6'6" twin-fin
fishtail

1975
8'0" pintail gun

1977
twin-fin

1980
6'2" updated
single-fin hotdogger

1981-now
modern three-fin
Thruster

Wiping out— it can be painful, but sometimes it's spectacular.

Getting "Tubed"

CHAPTER THREE

Once you own your own surfboard, it's time to tame the wild surf. If you're a beginner, take your time to learn the basic skills of surfing first before going on to the hot moves. A lot depends on how much time you want to spend training. Do you want to just have fun? Or do you want to become a professional surfer like Kelly Slater and Dino Andino someday?

First of all, you have to build up stamina. Surfing takes a lot of energy and strength, and surfers need to be able to recover from fatigue. Every time you go surfing, you'll be working your arm and back muscles, and your lungs. Every time you wipe out, you'll be using a great deal of energy in just fighting the water. So get yourself into shape.

Before you dive into the surf, you must be physically fit and know how to handle your board properly.

You should also be an excellent swimmer. Swimming in the ocean is different from swimming in a pool or a lake. It takes a lot of strength to dodge waves and swim underwater. As a guideline, beginners should be able to:

• Swim a short distance at top speed.

• Swim a long distance at a slower, steady pace.

• Remain underwater for at least 20 seconds.

• Have the strength to paddle his or her surfboard through at least two sets of breaking waves.

Now it's time to become familiar with your board.

To figure out whether your left or right foot should be forward once you are riding your board, run a short distance on dry land and then slide on a smooth surface. Which foot is in front? If it's your right foot, it's almost certainly better for you to do your surfing with your right foot forward. If it's your left foot, then you're a left-foot-first surfer. Those who surf with their left foot forward are called *regular* foot, and those who surf with their right foot forward are called *goofy* foot.

Whether you're a regular foot or goofy foot, the hardest part of surfing is learning how to stand on your board. Practice the standing movements. To get to this position, you will either come directly to your feet in one smooth motion or rise to your knees in a crouch and then stand up. Your legs, arms and hands will help balance you. Your feet should be spread about eight inches apart or less. The rear foot is turned at almost a right angle to the center line of the board. The body, of course, faces forward.

Launching Your Board

So much for training on dry land. Now you need to actually experience the ocean and learn the art of surfing by observing other surfers. Watch how they balance themselves on the board. Check out their stance and body movements. That's how you want to look when you finally hit the waves.

Practice the basics of paddling and board control before trying to catch your first wave. Take lessons if you can. Stay with an experienced surfer. Before you enter the ocean, check the water and waves. Is the bottom rocky or sandy? Is there a drop-off into deep water? Will breaking waves push you back to the beach? Are there any strong underwater channels that may cause you trouble? Check the lifeguard tower for the warning flags: Red is for dangerous conditions. Is there a surf warning posted?

The most frightening part of surfing is judging your distance from a set of waves. If you're too close to a wave when it's about to break, you can be thrashed. Sometimes a surfer can get caught in a set of big waves or an undertow. If he or she can paddle long and hard, it will be enough to avoid being pushed back to the shore or wiped out.

Get used to the water temperature. Go in slowly. Get the feel of your surfboard in shallow water before paddling out beyond the breakers. Try to relax. After a short time, your body will feel more comfortable. Even strong waves will seem easier once you've learned to adjust to the new setting.

As you walk out through small breaking surf, hold your board high. Rest it on your head or high under your arm and let the waves pass under it. Keep the nose of the board from dipping into the water or a wave will tear it from your grip. Always keep the board pointed straight ahead.

When you are in water above your knees, lie on your board with your head facing forward. The easiest position from which to paddle is the prone position. Hold your head up so you can see the oncoming waves. This also helps arch your back so that more muscles are brought into play when you stroke. Your arms, shoulders and back will work together, and their combined power can make your board go surprisingly fast and far.

To paddle out beyond the breakers, use a stroke that comes naturally. Dip your hands and arms into the water and pull back and through. Take long, strong strokes. Keep your body relaxed. Don't tense up. Once you're in position, turn your board around and wait for a wave that's just the right size for your ability.

You may have to go through or under waves as they move toward you. This takes a lot of practice. As a wave begins to break, dive beneath it by pushing your board under the whitewash to get to the outside break.

Waves generally come in sets, with pauses between every dozen waves or so. Storms at sea and offshore winds can produce rapidly changing conditions.

Catching a Wave

When a monster wave comes your way, timing is critical. Wait for the wave and then begin to paddle until it "takes hold" of you and your board. If you're a beginner, stay on your stomach for the ride. As you get better, move to your knees, and then, eventually, to your feet. Do what comes naturally, but try different stances. Watch the other surfers. Every ride will add to your education.

You never know what to expect when you catch a wave. A lot can happen. That's part of the excitement. The white water of a large wave can cover you completely and then seem to pass you by. You could wipe out. But if you keep your balance, you can sizzle, slash, carve and cut by shifting the positions of your feet, your body, your arms and hands. It's all a matter of balance. If you do not like the wave at all and want to pull out, make a sharp turn and steer your board back into the face of the wave. At the same time, try to come up and over the lip of the wave. It's a difficult movement, but with practice you should get the hang of it. You can end your ride one of two other ways: either wipe out, or fall away from your board and into the water. Another option is to stall your board by shuffling back to the rear holding the nose high in the air.

Naturally, some days are better surfing days than others. There are times when the surf is practically nonexistent and other times a storm will cause swells as high as 10 feet. It's a hurry up and wait game. You rush out with your board and wait for the perfect wave. Sometimes it shows up and sometimes it doesn't. But in the end, your patience will pay off and your reward will come in the form of a ride that really rips.

Sooner or later the only way to get the feel of surfing is to just do it.

Popular surfing areas can become overcrowded, so be sure to yield the right of way to someone who's already on the wave.

Rules of Conduct

As with every sport, there are certain rules of courtesy that should be obeyed. They help protect yourself and others, and make your time in the ocean more enjoyable.

- Avoid getting in the way of other surfers.
- The person riding the wave has the right of way.
- Never surf beyond your abilities.
- Keep yourself and your equipment in tip-top shape.
- Keep an eye out for swimmers.
- Don't force a surfer to drop out of a wave.

Always have a friend with you when you go surfing just in case you get in trouble or need help. Never surf alone. The ocean is a big, powerful force and can be very dangerous.

Watch out for underwater currents. Should you become caught in one, don't try to fight it. Simply drift along until it weakens to a point where you can swim toward the beach. Don't forget that the ocean is a natural home for living creatures of all shapes and sizes. Although shark attacks are rare, they do happen. If you spot the familiar fin, yell out a warning to others in the water and head for shore as quickly and calmly as you can. Practice caution at all times.

There are a number of thrills that come with surfing as you improve your skills and move up to more difficult maneuvers. For the most part, these new techniques are simply a mixed bag of tricks based on the fundamentals of surfing. First you should learn a few of the easier moves, as you need to be a pretty good surfer to attempt the following stunts.

Backside/Frontside Trim or Turn. These terms refer to your stance on the surfboard and which rail you are angling into the wave. If you're riding with your back to the wave, you're backside. If you're riding while facing the wave, you're frontside. This has a lot to do with whether you're a regular foot or a goofy foot.

Bottom Turn. As you come down the face of the wave, you might find yourself with no place to go. A bottom turn is a basic change in direction from down the face of the wave to back up toward the lip.

Cutback. If you hit a part of the wave that seems too slow, you can always cut back. This move is another basic change turn, except it's done so sharply that you almost completely reverse direction. Some surfers like to use this move to bank off the foam or the lip of a wave.

Off the Lip. This is just what it sounds like: You ride the board up the face of the wave and then take off from the top of the wave. To bank off the lip, simply pick a sweet spot that's about to break and shred the whitecap. With a lot of practice, you should be able to continue down the face of the wave as it heads for the beach.

Tube Riding. This is the ultimate pleasure in surfing. The secret is to hide yourself in the tube beneath the breaking lip or curl of the wave, then come back out for the next maneuver of your ride. If done correctly, a curtain of water will fall all around you. But if you get caught inside the tube, the water will crush you and cause you to wipe out.

Wipeout — A term used by surfers to indicate that moment when a wave hits you and forces you off your board and into the water.

Tom Carroll demonstrates a bottom turn (a), then goes off the lip (b,c) and then makes a cutback (d).

1 Paddle hard toward the wave. Shift your weight forward.

DUCK DIVING

Duck diving allows the force of the wave to pass overhead so you can continue paddling toward the spot where you want to catch the waves.

As the wave passes over you, thrust the nose forward and then ease up to the surface.

2 Use your weight to sink the nose.

3 Push the tail down with one foot.

4 Release your foot and let the nose tilt toward the surface.

CENTER OF GRAVITY

Turning and maintaining trim requires shifting your body's center of gravity. Moving your weight closer to your board will make it accelerate: standing more erect ("unweighting") will slow or stall your board.

STANCE

Maintaining a wide stance on your board to distribute your weight evenly will make it easier to maneuver and help prevent you from being knocked off.

WATCH THE NOSE

Always keep an eye on the nose of your board in critical situations.

SPEED   Doing tricks is easier when you have as much speed as possible.

How would you like to surf a wave this high?

Surf's Up

CHAPTER FOUR

You may come to a point in your surfing career when you will want to enter some kind of contest. As your skills improve, you'll want to test yourself against other surfers. Some of the world champions are young and have only a few years of experience. Who knows? You could be next.

Competitions aren't hard to find. Local and national organizations hold contests around the country. Of course, many of these will be far from where you live. It's fun to travel to exotic playgrounds and test your surfing skills against the best.

For example, Shane Beschen, age 21, has traveled to Australia, France and South Africa—all within a couple of months. He recently flew to Mozambique in search of the perfect wave for a surfing film. "Most of it was a nightmare of boredom," he told a reporter. "But we did find some really good waves."

Beschen is the top-ranked rookie on the Association of Surfing Professionals (ASP) World Tour. He finished second on the California-based Bud Surf Tour in 1991 and won the championship in 1992. Although he has yet to go to college, he has managed to keep his balance on life. He knows he can go it alone in the world, and he's beginning to appreciate the education he has received from his travels.

If you're an amateur, look for something a little closer to home. Once you become good enough to win money, you can turn pro. The prize money you win can help pay for trips all over the world.

One of the first major events in surfing was the Duke Kahanamoku Invitational Surfing Championships held on the Hawaiian island of Oahu in

Professional surfing tournaments have become big spectator events.

1965. The waves were awesome that day, according to several newspaper accounts. In fact, one surfing magazine described the event as "surfing's greatest competitive event ever." It was the first pro contest ever held and featured 24 of the world's finest surfers. The action was broadcast on television to an estimated 50 million people.

Today, there are more than 400 professional surfers in the United States alone. Worldwide, pro surfers hail from countries such as Australia, Brazil and Japan. Perhaps one day you'll enter a surfing contest that will be seen on television. You never know what the future has in store if you make up your mind to work hard and go for the glory.

The Big Time

A young surfer always starts out as an amateur. In Southern California, for example, schools have surfing teams just like their basketball or football teams. Competitions are held every month. Every day surfers of all ages can be seen practicing their skills in the water from Aliso Creek to Zuma Beach.

Competitive surfing is fun to watch, and each year it seems the skill level of the surfers rises sharply. If you want to compete against the best in the world, you will have to spend a lot of time practicing. In fact, becoming a professional surfer is almost a full-time job.

Wendy Botha, just one of the many fine women surfers on the pro circuit.

The brave surfers who survive Hawaii's Pipeline earn both prize money and glory.

Several organizations sponsor professional surfing contests. One of the most important is the ASP, a nonprofit organization that promotes surfing events around the world. It was founded in 1983 when it replaced the older International Professional Surfing Tour.

Anyone can join the ASP, including amateur surfers. All it takes is an application and a little hustle. In exchange, the ASP provides a scoring system, judging, and ratings for surfers and event promoters. It holds championship contests in men's, women's, and longboard divisions. Each division has two levels of competition: the World Qualifying Series of 30 to 40 events throughout the year, and the World Championship Tour of 10 to 12 events. This two-level system gives surfers more chances at prize money. They compete in several rounds of one-on-one competition to determine a champion for each individual event. The surfer who has won the most points at the end of the year is considered the World Champion.

Stops on the circuit include Australia, Africa, the United States, Europe, Japan, Brazil, and the December grand finale off the Hawaiian Islands—otherwise known as The Pipeline Masters. This is one of the premier events of the year. The surf gets up to around 15 to 20 feet, and it's "incredible to watch," according to Meg Bernardo, U.S. Manager for the Association of Surfing Professionals.

Surfers must enter the qualifying series to assure a spot on the World Championship Tour. An unlimited number of events are scheduled throughout the year. One such tour series is the Bud Pro Tour. It features both the Pro-Am Surfing Division and the Easy Rider Bodyboarding Division. All heats consist of four competitors and range in length from 20 minutes for the trials to 30 minutes for the finals.

Contestants who want to win must always be on their toes. The pace of a contest is fast. They must constantly check the beach for signals regarding their heat. The announcer, for example, informs them of their wave count and interference calls. The timekeeper uses horns and colored flags. One horn blast followed by a green flag signifies the start of a heat; two successive blasts followed by a yellow flag signifies the five-minute warning. And one blast followed by a red flag signifies the end of a heat.

If you snooze, you lose.

But the real battle of surfing competitions is overcoming your fears and being able to catch the "biggest and best waves" in the shortest amount of time, says Ian Cairns, director of the Bud Surf Tour.

When you learn how to surf you have unlimited time to catch as many waves or as few waves as you want. A surfer can be out in the water for three hours and catch only one great wave. But in surfing competitions, surfers have 20 minutes to catch four to six good waves. When the surf is large, the competition is between the rider and the waves. "Your fears are justified under these conditions because the waves you're facing are life-threatening," says Cairns. "When the surf is small, it's a matter of who can do the best hot-dog surfing. It's a lot more competitive."

Some surfers become famous for their hot maneuvers, but they don't have good competitive records. They mostly surf for themselves. Other surfers are simply great competitors. "There are so many free spirits in the surfing world, that some of them are simply unable to adjust to the competition," says Cairns. "They remain great surfers, but they'll never learn how to compete well. We call these guys 'soul surfers' because they surf only for themselves.

"Every surfer eventually reaches a crossroads," adds Cairns. "They can choose to take the competitive road, or they can become soul surfers. But the escape that comes with surfing is with 100 percent of the athletes. That's something no surfer ever loses."

Surfing contestants are judged on how well they ride their waves for a given time period.

Judging a Contest

The typical surfing contest is judged by a panel of five pros. These judges give each surfer a score of 1 to 10, based on how well they think the surfer performed. They look for rides that are exciting and surfers who push the limits of surfing in a controlled manner. A single round of competition is usually between 25 and 30 minutes, depending on wave conditions. "This allows the surfers to express their style," says Bernardo.

The Bud Pro Tour's philosophy on judging is simple: What is the most exciting and who is pushing the limits of surfing in a controlled manner? In the Pro-Am Surfing Division, the surfer who completes "the most radical maneuvers using speed and power on the largest waves" will usually be named winner. The judges typically leave room for surfers to express their own unique style. Every ride is scored, and the results are then tallied.

Prize Money

One reason surfers enter contests is because of the prize money. Winners can earn anywhere from $10,000 to $150,000, not including sponsorships, which can double or triple their earnings. For example, pro surfer Dino Andino won the U.S. Championship in 1990, then joined the world tour. Since then he has earned hundreds of thousands in prize money and endorsements.

These high stakes make today's surfing very competitive. In the early days of the sport, money wasn't the reason for entering a contest—winning was more an issue of prestige and personal pride.

In the winter of 1969, first place prize money for the Fifth Annual Duke Kahanamoku Hawaiian Surfing Classic was only $1,000. Then, in 1970, Hawaiian surfer-businessman Fred Hemmings came up with $6,000 for the first Smirnoff Pro-Am meet. Surfers from all parts of the world arrived to compete for a $3,000 first-place prize. It was carried away by Nat Young, an aggressive power-surfer from Australia.

Today, winners are paid in cash. But the real money to be made in pro surfing comes from endorsements. Surfers are contracted by manufacturers of surfing gear and other products to endorse their line. Kelly Slater, for example, has already earned more than $1 million this way.

Surfing is a sport that will give you lifelong satisfaction.

An Endless Summer

C H A P T E R   F I V E

After you've sharpened your skills as a surfer, you might want to think about going to some of the other exotic playgrounds. The island of Oahu, Hawaii, for example, is a killer spot for high-performance surfing—especially the north shore. It's a dream destination for most surfers where waves can get as high as 60 feet because of the strong winds. Pipeline is one of the North Shore's best known beaches, and Sandy Beach is another because the waves break with big tubes and steep faces.

A great surfing location on the United States mainland is the "Wedge" in Newport Beach, California. The waves here bounce off a rock jetty at the harbor and slam back into oncoming waves, making for even bigger waves. In September and October the waves are spectacular.

Other favorite surfing areas in California include Huntington Beach, Laguna Beach and San Clemente, where the waves are gentle and smooth and can make for a long ride.

If you don't live in Hawaii or California, you can practice your skills in other places like Florida, for example. Daytona Beach and the Cape Canaveral area often have good surf. Virginia Beach, Virginia, and Ocean City, Maryland, can also come through with pretty big waves. Even the New Jersey Shore and Long Island in New York have especially good conditions for surfing.

So whether you live on the East Coast or the West Coast, you can always find some place to surf. But what if you don't live near the ocean?

Windsurfing is a lot like ocean surfing, only without the waves. You still have a board, usually about ten feet long and three feet wide. And you still have to balance yourself while standing on the board. But instead of strong waves

BODYBOARDING

There are a lot of other water sports besides surfing that will give you thrills and excitement.

Bodyboarding, for example, is similar to surfing only instead of standing on a board, you lie on your belly on a short, flexible board. You can still go sliding down the face of a wave with all the intensity of a surfer, but your hands and elbows are used to maneuver the board instead of your legs and feet.

Like surfboards, bodyboards come in different sizes, shapes and colors. Some have rounded noses, some have blunt noses, some have square tails, and some have curved tails. You'll also need swim fins to help you gain enough speed to catch a wave.

For your first try at bodyboarding, find a beach with a smooth, sandy shore and gentle waves. Stay away from rocks and reefs, and save the big waves for later when you've mastered the basic skills.

Unlike surfing, you can bodyboard almost anywhere. Wave pools are good sources of practice water if you don't live near a beach. These are giant swimming holes with a machine at one end that makes waves up to four feet or higher. Only a few wave pools, however, allow bodyboarders to use their facilities.

pushing you along, the wind propels you by means of a sail that you hold upright on the board. You can windsurf on lakes, ponds, bays, and rivers—any place where there's wind and water.

Windsurfing was invented by surfer Hoyle Schweitzer and Jim Drake. Both men liked sailboats and surfing. One day in 1967 when surfing conditions were poor, Hoyle figured out a way to attach a sail to a surfboard. To his surprise, he ended up gliding along the water's surface like a bird. Just like that, the sport of windsurfing was born.

As with surfing, it takes a while to get used to the board. At first, you will fall into the water a lot. Windsurfing looks easy but, like surfing, it's not. You can learn to windsurf by taking classes or by practicing and watching other windsurfers. If you do try to windsurf, you'll no doubt hear phrases like *raise the sail*, *sheet in* and *sheet out*, *steer the boat*, and *tack* and *jibe*. It's important to understand these movements.

You raise the sail by grabbing the rope attached to the sail and pulling it into a ready position to catch the wind. You sheet in and sheet out by allowing the sail to catch the wind. As you pull the sail more into the wind, it becomes harder to hold. It's time to either sheet out or let the sail go slack.

Windsurfing offers board riders a different challenge—employing a sail to maneuver over any body of water where there's wind.

Once you become a surfer, you will never be far from the waves.

You steer the board by using the tools at your disposal: the wind, the mast, and the sail. It works because the wind pushes the sail assembly, and thus pushes you and your board. Once you're on the move, it's important to know how to tack and jibe, which allow you to make U-turns. You tack by turning the boat into the wind. you jibe by turning the boat with the wind.

There are many factors that make windsurfing a difficult sport: wind speed, steering, and making turns. With practice you can overcome these hurdles. Of course, no windsurfer can go as fast as the wind because of the drag of the water on the board. Still, some riders go sailing at between 35 and 45 miles per hour.

As with surfing, you always want to exercise caution. Be sure you wear the appropriate clothing. If the water's cold, wear a wet suit. If you're not a good swimmer, be sure to wear a life jacket. If the water is too rough or the wind is too strong, or if you're tired, be sure to take a breather and rest on the shore.

A Surfer's Paradise

Surfing has always held the promise of endless summers, fun and romance. A surfer's only concerns seem to be good waves and good times, making the lifestyle all that more attractive. Surfers love exotic playgrounds like Indonesia, South Africa, France, Australia, Hawaii and the coast of California. You'll always find the wet suit crowd where the surf is really spectacular.

Surfers set their own styles and live by their own rules. They tend to look for perfect waves, and they never stay in one place too long. Surfers are free-thinking individuals, and that's reflected in how they live. They have an intimate—sometimes inspiring and frightening—relationship with nature, and that defines their attitude toward life.

Surfers get to carry on with their education without the help of a teacher. Their classroom is the open road. "You can learn a lot from surfing," says Cairns. "Seeing the world and learning about other cultures is an education you can't find in any classroom."

The sport of surfing has created a lifestyle unknown to most people. But surfers wouldn't have it any other way. They've had to suffer long and hard to achieve the ultimate in surfing pleasure, and their rewards are well deserved.

Glossary

Air-whipping. A style of surfing where the rider attempts to get airborne.

Backside. A surfing maneuver where the surfer has his back to the wave.

Barrel. The round hollow space that forms when a wave breaks.

Bodyboard. A short, flexible board that you lie on to ride the waves.

Bottom turn. A basic change in direction when surfing from down the face of the wave to back up toward the lip.

Breaker. A wave that breaks into foam against the shore.

Carve. A term used to describe the art of surfing.

Current. Underwater channels in the ocean.

Cut. A term used to describe the art of surfing.

Cutback. A sharp change in direction while surfing.

Deck. The top portion of a surfboard that the rider stands on.

Face. The front side of a wave.

Fiberglas. A hard but flexible glass-like material used to build surfboards.

Frontside. A surfing maneuver where the surfer rides while facing the wave.

Goofy foot. A surfer who surfs with his left foot forward.

Jibe. A windsurfing term that means to turn the board with the wind.

Kickboard. A short, flexible board used to practice kicking in the water.

Lip. The crest on top of a wave.

Longboard. A long surfboard.

Off the lip. A surfing maneuver where the rider banks off the crest of the wave.

Rails. The rounded edges of a surfboard.

Raise the sail. A windsurfing term that means to grab the rope attached to the sail and pull it into a ready position.

Right foot. A surfer who surfs with his right foot forward.

Sheet in. A windsurfing term that means to position the sail to catch the wind.

Sheet out. A windsurfing term that means to let the sail go slack.

Shred. A term used to describe the art of surfing.

Sizzle. A term used to describe the art of surfing.

Skeg. A plastic rudder or fin on the bottom of a surfboard that lends stability and gives the rider the ability to do more tricks.

Slash. A term used to describe the art of surfing.

Swell. A long, rolling wave or series of waves.

Tack. A windsurfing term that means to turn the board into the wind.

Tide. The rising and falling of the ocean surface.

Tri-fin. Three skegs on the bottom of a surfboard.

Tube. Another term for the round, hollow space that forms when a wave breaks.

Tube riding. The ultimate pleasure in surfing, when the rider hides inside the tube or barrel of a wave.

Trench. The dip in the water just in front of a wave.

Wet suit. A skin-tight covering that helps keep the body warm in cold water.

White water. A frothy water that forms after a wave breaks on shore.

Wipeout. A surfing term that indicates the moment when a wave hits you and forces you off your board and into the water.

For Additional Information

Association of Surfing Professionals
P.O. Box 309
Huntington Beach, CA 92648
(714) 892-8826

Bud Surf Tour
530 Sixth Street
Hermosa Beach, CA 90254
(310) 372-0414

Eastern Surfing Association
11 Adams Point Road
Barrington, RI 02806
(407) 728-4325

Hawaii Surfing Association
3107 Lincoln Avenue
Honolulu, HI 96816
(808) 737-0231

National Scholastic Surfing Association
P.O. Box 495
Huntington Beach, CA 92648
(714) 536-0445

Surfer Magazine
P.O. Box 1028
Dana Point, CA 92629
(714) 496-5922

Surfing Magazine
P.O. Box 3010
San Clemente, CA 92674
(714) 492-7873.

The United States Surfing Federation
7104 Island Village Drive
Long Beach, CA 90803
(310) 596-7785

Western Surfing Association
7104 Island Village Drive
Long Beach, CA 90803
(310) 662-4610

Other good books to read about surfing are:

Surfing: The Ultimate Pleasure by Leonard Lueras. New York: Workman Publishing, 1984.

Surfing: Basic Techniques by Arnold Madison. New York: David McKay Company, Inc., 1979.

Surfing: How to Improve Your Technique by Mark Sufrin. New York: Franklin Watts, Inc., 1973.

Index

Alter, Hobie, 15
Andino, Dino, 21
Association of Surfing Professionals (ASP), 31, 35

Ballard, Rochelle, 8
Beschen, Shane, 8, 31
Blake, Tom, 13-14
bodyboard(ing), 13, 40
Burridge, Pam, 8

Cairns, Ian, 35-36
Carroll, Nick, 11

Drake, Jim, 40

Freeth, George, 8

Garcia, Sunny, 8

Hardman, Damien, 8
Huntington Beach International Surfing Museum, 15

Kahanamoku, Duke, 8-10
Kahanamoku Invitational Surfing Championships, 31-32
kickboard, 13

longboards, 15

Osborne, Vanessa, 8

Pipeline, 35, 39

Quigg, Joe, 14
Schweitzer, Hoyle, 40

Simmons, Robert, 11, 14
Slater, Kelly, 8, 21
soul surfers, 36
surfboard(s)
    choosing, 15
    cost, 15

designers, 14, 15
Fiberglas, 11, 13, 14
first, 13
hollow, 13
leash, 17
polyurethane, 15
shapes, 14, 19 (illus.)
size, 13
steering, 14
Styrofoam, 14
weight, 14
surfing
    and balance, 24
    catching a wave, 23-24
    checking conditions, 22
    compared with skateboarding, 6
    competitions, 31-37
    duck diving, 28-29
    with foot straps, 19
    learning, 21-29
    origins, 8
    outlaw sport, 11
    with paddling gloves, 17
    popular spots, 39
    prize money, 37
    riding foot, 22
    rules, 25
    and swimming ability, 21
    tricks, 26
tube riding, 6

wave(s)
    choosing, 8, 23-24
    height, 24
    swell, 6
    types, 8
wax, 17
wetsuit(s), 11, 17
windsurfing
    boards, 39-40
    maneuvers, 40, 43
    origins, 40
    precautions, 43